Microbes

Living Things

There are microbes

in the water.

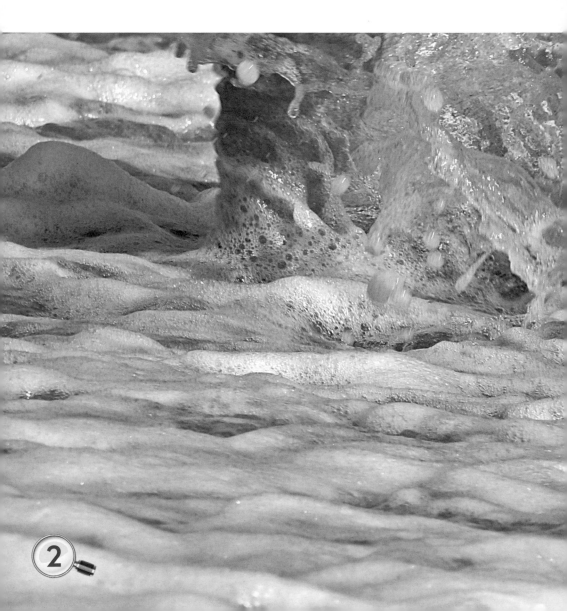

There are microbes
in the grass.

There are microbes
in the dirt.

There are microbes
in the mud.

There are microbes in the bread.

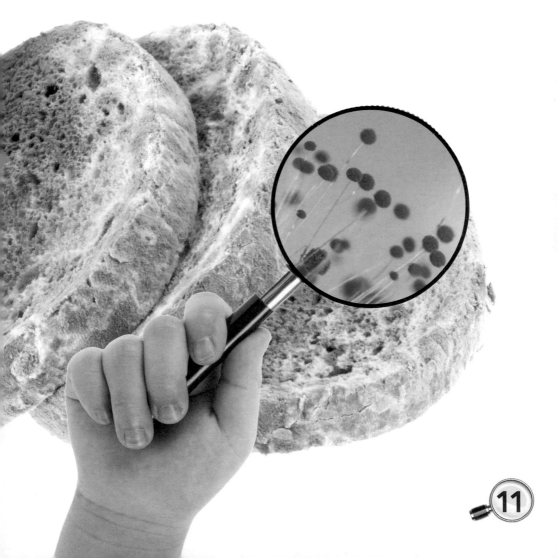

There are microbes
in the cheese.

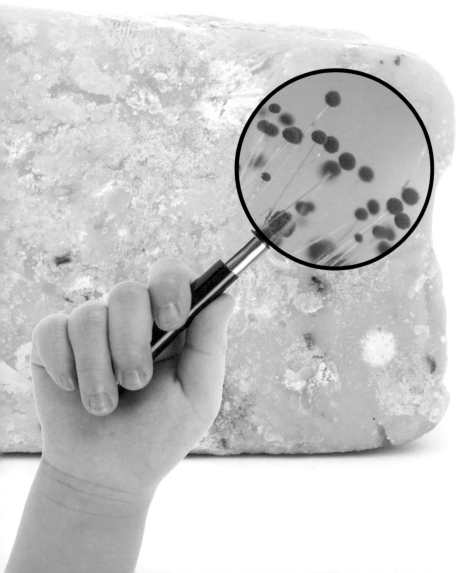

13

There are microbes
on the swing.

There are microbes on me, too.